Dreamy
Snippets

Dreamy Snippets

ELIZABETH CANNON

ISBN 978-0-578-94252-0 (Paperback Edition)

Library of Congress Cataloging-in-Publication Data

Names: Cannon, Elizabeth, author.
Title: Dreamy Snippets / Elizabeth Cannon.
Description: Tennesee: Lightning Source
Identifiers: LCCN 2021914187 (print) |
ISBN 978-0-578-94252-0 (paperback)

Excerpt from gold leaf-yellow-wall-texture image: Freepik.com. This book of illustrations has been designed using resources from Freepik.com. Reprinted with permission.

Editing by Luna Beasley
Cover design by Shamim Sarkar

Printed and bound in the United States of America
First printing, 2021

Published by IngramSpark®
1 Ingram Blvd.
La Vergne, TN 37086

Visit ThatElizabeth.com

I am an artist

A fire burns within me

Please help me embrace this flame

So that it may become transparent

For the world to see

What I am

CONTENTS

ESCAPE

I need to take a trip,

To go to a place where the grass is green, the sky is blue.

Where only sounds of chirping birds are heard

Or ocean tides rolling onto a sandy beach.

Perhaps the sound of a church bell in a land

I've never been before.

I know why now; the reason

behind my love for nature all these years.

Such adventures take us away

from life's disappointments.

From all the loud noises of a bustling and chaotic world.

MYSTICAL

I heard the wind howling this evening.

I felt something, a vague memory of this exact feeling.

Back then, I could find a name for it,

So why can't I seem to find my words now?

Sometimes, I work best with the windows wide open

on stormy nights.

It floods my mind with inspiration to write.

THE UNKNOWN

The moon looks so high up,

Shining brighter than the dreary clouds

dancing in the foreground.

It lightens up the sky in a way that's so calm,

Yet frightful on a night like this.

A night where the wind howls and courses to and fro.

It messes with my hair that's down to my waist,

The trees uncontrollably throwing things in my direction.

But they miss

Because the unknown protected me on this night.

MONOPOLY

I love games,

and I'm very competitive when playing them.

But this game you see isn't like the rest.

This one... I no longer wish to be part of.

You're the Banker, and I'm the Shoe.

I'm in Jail; you're on Go.

Set me free, set me free.

You said you would,

But I'm only walking in circles with you.

I need you to land on my hotels, Park Place, and Boardwalk

Then it's game over.

THE NECKLACE

Tonight, I wear a little bit of hope around my neck.

Throughout my sleep, I shall wear

And throughout tomorrow, I shall wear

Because the time is near

for my dear son to spend several nights away from me.

He's just a baby!

How do I stand on my own two feet without stumbling?

How do I speak without screaming from the agony

filling my heart and lungs?

My reactions and prayers are my only abilities.

And then something whispers in my ear

But loud enough for all my cells to hear:

'Trust the process.'

This, too, shall pass.

WONDROUS

Look around.

Aren't you inspired?

Aren't you awed?

Aren't you blown away by all that is here?

By all that is present?

See for yourself if you have not:

Seen the wind blow

Rays from the sunlight,

Or heard the howling beyond the mountaintops,

The gracefulness in dancers,

The art in artists,

And the knowledge belonging to the power of the wise.

Breathe in the air,

Exhale,

Touch the sand,

Feel the water.

All that is, all that will be, is all that ever was.

ENLIGHTENMENT

I had an epiphany,

This eureka moment.

It was only for a split second,

As though I'd uncovered the essence of life itself.

I must grab the materials I ought to use

To capture this fading insight and stitch it into a necklace,

A piece of jewelry to have as my constant reminder

To have by my side,

Like a pet dog to his owner.

Oh, how I can't wait for the sun to rise.

I love a fresh start...

...the awakening of the soul.

It's quite refreshing, to say the least.

THE OTHER SIDE

An empty bed, still sunken from where you slept.

I am living proof of the strength it takes to overcome

Love, betrayal, and death.

I have spent enough nights sleeping on my side

since the day you left.

I have crossed over the ocean to the lands awaiting me.

I have filled the gap between yin and yang.

I am the bridge to my own success and happiness.

There I am,

Now comfortable on what is no longer

Your side of the bed.

STEALER

Why must there be death?

What awaits beyond the living?

Death is like the sound of rain on a black night.

It rains and rains, tears of a shattered heart.

Then utter silence fills the sky

while grey clouds hang low.

Somber faces in the distance, their bodies filled with grief.

There are no words to soothe them.

Death raided on this stormy night,

Like a knight in shining armor.

But instead of coming to the rescue,

It came to steal.

And nobody could see it but for a few.

Death took away the lives of loved ones,

Leaving them in despair.

How awful it seems; yet, life goes on.

PIERCING EYES

After nearly bumping into one another,

There stood a man

with good posture and strong legs.

His eyes pulled me in for a rested glance.

He apologized swiftly with a gentleman-like kindness

in his heart.

A smile spread across my face,

And a lightness formed in my feet.

For an instant, I felt I could fly, like all those rare moments

in my dreams.

I felt like a woman again,

Like I could do anything.

Though the feeling lasted less than a minute,

The thoughts remain.

Who was this person who made me feel this way?

THE SOUL SEARCH

What do you want most?

Money to spend or to save?

Is it money to spend now

or is it to put away and spend later?

Is it to eat pizza, go to the movies or concerts,

To buy clothes?

Or is it to travel the world, to Israel, the Holy Land?

Perhaps Ireland, China, or Japan.

What do you truly want?

Focus.

You must do what your heart is calling you to do.

Follow your heart, soul, mind, and strength.

Willpower is underrated.

Choose and go.

Find your life's work and own it.

Breathe in the sun-filled air, full of life and light

and awe-inspiring opportunities...

...they await you.

Be one with your mind, body, and spirit.

Love all that you are, love all that is present.

You do not need certain clothes to wear

or jewelry to be bought.

You do not need to make a statement out of fashion,

For what you want is not in things.

You know this.

What you desire is living the dream, your dream life.

You can have that if you truly want it.

You will work hard now and find a way to make it happen.

NATURE

The sound of chirping birds and joyous leaves.

Tranquility all around.

Earthy tones, good lighting during the day,

and mysterious treasures at night.

At dusk, the sounds of crickets and frogs

are music to my soul while my body drifts off to sleep.

Then when the light touches the Earth's surface,

spreading its wings across the sky,

It's smoother than the butter

I spread on my breakfast toast.

LIBERATION

I love the singsong of the birds.

It makes my heart free

and my chest dance with every breath,

Like the waves of an ocean.

PATIENCE

I am an amateur artist.

The thing I lack is patience.

You see, some days I get what I like to call

'the artist's splurge.'

Better put in simpler terms,

There are days where the desire to create

from a vast range of mediums appears

all in one day.

And it's that day when several masterpieces are born.

When the sun goes down,

I dream of waking up the next morning with an

incredible amount of talent

far exceeding my capabilities.

But I wake only to find that it's hope.

Don't get me wrong — there's a lot of power in hope alone.

But my desired skill level is so far-fetched

that it could not possibly become just that

over the course of one winter night.

Or could it?

I do believe in the power of the unknown.

Nevertheless, patience is my enemy at this point.

I'm trying to become friends with it.

The best we can do is practice

Until patience rewards us through deserving.

FEAR AT ITS FINEST

I wonder if all married men and women are happy.

Why do they stay together if they're unhappy?

Maybe they stay together because, deep down,

they're afraid of being alone.

Or perhaps they have children with that other person.

Maybe it's that they love the feeling of being loved

Or that they're afraid they may end up alone forever.

Maybe they're afraid because they don't know what it's like

to be on the other side,

Even though they were doing it long before any relationship.

They don't remember what it's like

to cooperate on their own again, as a single person,

a single mother, father, etcetera.

Whatever the case may be,

I hope they gain the courage and strength

to be honest with themselves if they are miserable.

A lot of us are quick to settle down, selling ourselves short.

Sigh. If you doubt your circumstances right now...

Then it's going to take guts to walk away.

I can't say how many because, in my case,

The tables turned on me.

But don't lose hope; we are not all the same people.

Because, man oh man, are we capable of living

the happiest, healthiest,

most productive, most flourishing lives ahead of us.

...if only we weren't afraid.

CONQUER

Can't stop, won't stop.

Oh yes, the famous line.

But I'm creating a new saying

for the go-getters and the ambitious,

for the adventurers and the seekers.

This one will be a new line

For those who know that anything is possible when you believe.

It goes like this:

'Can stop, will stop any unnecessary hindrances

until I reach my goals.'

MAXED-OUT

Words

They come to me in either two forms:

As fast as the speed of light

Or slow, like this chocolate pudding

running down the side of my mug.

I now see how having huge debt

can drive people into depression.

It's a burden.

But not just any burden—

It's the obligatory payback of what you owe

During a time when you don't have the means

to accomplish it.

I thought to myself, 'I'll figure it out.

But first, let me indulge in this hot pudding.'

BELIEVE

An old man once told me never to say
'I can't.'

Because I can.

It's rare that I meet someone as like-minded as I.

A free spirit; that's what I am.

I'm an artist, and I'm here to fulfill my life's work.

It's what I know I was called to do.

I can't lie to myself, so why should I lie to others?

I believe anyone can turn a passion, a talent of any kind,

Into a successful career.

BLANK

Sometimes, I feel alone on the darkest days

When the sun is not out.

I look around,

But all I see is empty space.

PARTING

Maryland,

The place where change happened

Like the destruction of an earthquake.

I've been to many places,

But none quite as painfully free as here.

I smile and close my eyes.

My favorite place ought to be that of the tides,

The cries of the seagulls, the bustling boardwalk.

I can still remember, as I stand here in the dead of winter

with no one around, the sounds of chatter and laughter.

I can see the smiles on people's faces.

My heart soars above the sea.

I watch as people celebrate the Fourth of July.

I bite my lip to hold back the pain of nostalgia.

But it's too late; my eyes glisten

Like the bright sunlight casting its glitter upon the water.

I breathe it all in—the salty air, the scenery.

I feel the wind of wondrous adventures

from every moment that passed,

The good times and the bad.

I will always be grateful for what has been.

And now I swallow my tears

To what has become the end of the book.

My feet feel heavy,

But slowly and surely,

they take one step, two steps onward,

Heading in a new direction

That will mark the beginning of a new life,

 a new chapter to a brand new book.

I won't forget you, Ocean City.

Farewell.